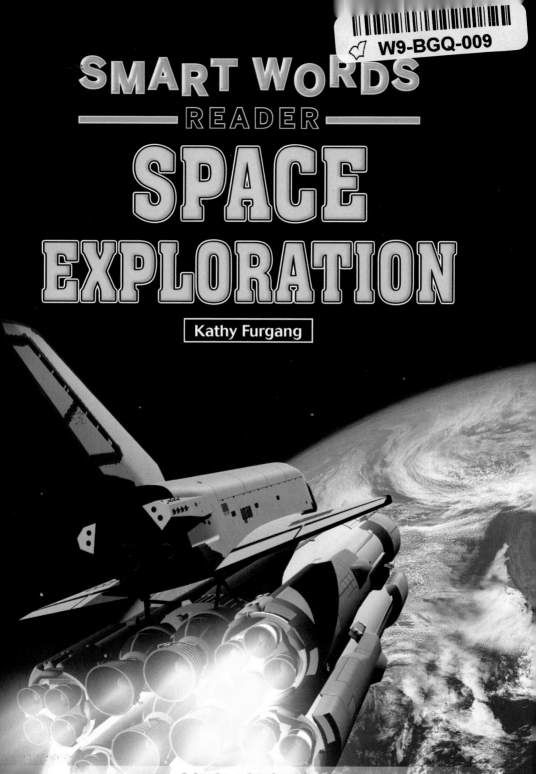

# SMART WORDS
## ─ READER ─
# SPACE EXPLORATION

Kathy Furgang

**SCHOLASTIC INC.**
New York  Toronto  London  Auckland
Sydney  Mexico City  New Delhi  Hong Kong

# What are SMART WORDS?

Smart Words are frequently used words that are critical to understanding concepts taught in the classroom. The more Smart Words a child knows, the more easily he or she will grasp important curriculum concepts. Smart Words Readers introduce these key words in a fun and motivational format while developing important literacy skills. Each new word is highlighted, defined in context, and reviewed. Engaging activities at the end of each chapter allow readers to practice the words they have learned.

**ISBN**  978-0-545-36826-1

**Packaged by Q2AMedia**

Copyright © 2012 by Scholastic Inc.

**Picture Credit:** t= top, b= bottom, l= left, r= right, c= center

Cover Page: Shutterstock
Title Page: Shutterstock
Content Page: P. Carril/ESA

4: NASA; 5t: Hulton Archive/Getty Images; 5b: Stuart Atkinson/NASA;
6: Patrick Shyu/Dreamstime; 7: HYPERLINK "http://www.gsfc.nasa.gov/"
Goddard Space Flight Center/NASA; 8: NASA; 9: NASA; 10: Toria/Shutterstock;
11: NASA; 13: NASA; 14: Jet Propulsion Laboratory/NASA; 15tl: Jochen Tack/
HYPERLINK "http://www.photolibrary.com/brands/?event-brands
.getBrandSearchPage&brandid=890" \t "parent" Imagebroker.net/Photolibrary;
15tr: J.Huart/ESA; 16: Hubblesite/NASA; 17: ESA and M. Livio and the Hubble 20th
Anniversary Team/Hubblesite/NASA; 18: Jet Propulsion Laboratory/NASA; 19: Jet
Propulsion Laboratory—Caltech/NASA; 20: HYPERLINK "http://www.spacetelescope
.org/" ESA and H.E. Bond/NASA; 21: Jet Propulsion Laboratory/NASA; 22: NASA;
23: NASA; 24-25: Chris Butler/Science Photo Library; 26-27: Tim Pyle/NASA;
28: Chris Butler/Science Photo Library; 29: NASA; 30-31: Bruce Rolff/Shutterstock.

12 11 10 9 8 7 6 5 4                    18 19 20 21 22/0

Printed in the U.S.A.                                        40
First printing, January 2012

# Table of Contents

# Chapter 1

# Mission — To the Moon!

*This is Apollo Saturn Launch Control:*

*The target for the* Apollo 11 *astronauts, the moon, will be a distance of 218,096 miles away at liftoff.*

*2... 1...0 ...all engines running. LIFTOFF!*

Liftoff!

It was July 16, 1969. The world watched the huge rocket go up high into the air. *Apollo 11* carried three men into space. Two of those men would be the first people to walk on the moon.

The *Saturn V* rocket lifts *Apollo 11* from Earth on its way to the moon.

## SMART WORDS

**astronomy**  the study of space and objects in space

**telescope**  a tool that makes faraway objects appear closer

Have you ever looked up into the sky and wondered what was beyond Earth? People have done this for a long time. Astronomy is one of the oldest sciences. **Astronomy** is the study of space and space objects.

In 1609, Galileo Galilei became the first person to look at the moon through a telescope. Three hundred sixty years later, Neil Armstrong would walk on the moon.

Would you like to see into space? A **telescope** makes faraway objects appear closer. This invention helps people see stars and planets. People have been using telescopes for over 400 years.

Astronaut Neil Armstrong, the first to step on the moon, described the moment as "one small step for man, one giant leap for mankind."

# Off Like a Rocket!

*BOOM!* A shower of red, yellow, and green light bursts across the night sky. The crowd *oohs* and *ahhs*. Sparkles seem to rain on the crowd. It's the Fourth of July! Many fireworks you have seen were shot from small **rockets**. In fact, fireworks are the oldest form of rockets.

SMART WORDS

**rocket**  a type of engine that burns fuel and pushes hot gases out one end to move

**force**  a push or pull that acts on an object

Rocket power is used for other things, too. Have you ever dreamed about space travel? Rockets have enough force to blast spacecraft with people on board into space. Space rockets are huge. The biggest — *Saturn V* — is 363 feet (111 meters) tall!

How do rockets work? Think about what happens when a balloon releases air. It shoots across the room! The escaping air is a **force** that pushes the balloon. Rockets burn fuel to create hot gas. The rocket engine pushes the hot gas out one end. This shoots the rocket upward. Liftoff!

Robert Goddard is known as the "Father of Rocketry." In 1902, he wrote a paper about the possibility of using rockets for space exploration — when he was a high-school student!

# To the Moon!

We have rockets that can blast into space. Where should we send them? To the moon! The moon is Earth's closest neighbor. We look up at it and see its surface. But what is it really like? How can we find out?

Rockets can take robots into space. A robot is a machine that can do tasks for people. People can tell the robot what to do from far away. Scientists sent robots to take pictures of the moon. They got information to make maps of the moon. Robots even picked up soil there! Scientists got a lot of great information from the robots.

This robot landed on the moon. It collected soil samples with its robotic arm.

Astronauts train to learn how to live in space.

The robots were first to the moon. But people soon followed. Who were these special people? An **astronaut** is a person trained to travel in space. Astronauts wear special gear for space travel. They also learn special skills.

The first astronauts who went to the moon were Neil Armstrong, Edwin "Buzz" Aldrin, and Michael Collins. They trained for a long time. They learned how to fly the spacecraft and how to walk on the moon. They learned how to live in space.

## SMART WORDS

**robot**   a machine that can do tasks for people

**astronaut**   a person who is trained to travel in space

# SMART WORDS

Match each description with the correct Smart Word.

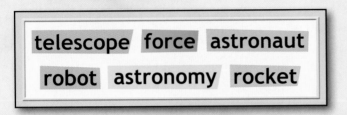

telescope force astronaut
robot astronomy rocket

1. a type of engine that burns fuel and pushes hot gases out one end to move

2. the study of space and objects in space

3. a push or pull that acts on an object

4. a person who is trained to travel in space

5. a tool that makes faraway objects appear closer

6. a machine that can do tasks for people

Answers on page 32

## Talk Like a Scientist

Draw pictures to show the different things people have used to explore space. Use your Smart Words to describe your pictures.

# SMART FACTS

## Did You Know?

Scientists used computers for the first trip to the moon. But today's smart phones are more powerful than those early computers!

## Incredible!

The spacecraft that took the astronauts to the moon lost a lot of its fuel. It had only 30 seconds of fuel left when it landed!

## Fascinating Fact

The moon has no weather. There is no wind to blow the soil. So the astronauts' footprints are still there today!

# Chapter 2

# All Aboard! Shuttling to Space

How do people travel to and from space? They take a **space shuttle**. A space shuttle is a spacecraft that takes people and cargo to and from space. NASA has launched shuttles into space more than 130 times.

A space shuttle is different from earlier spacecraft. A space shuttle rockets into space and docks at space stations. It cannot fly to, or land on, the moon. But it can land on Earth like an airplane! The earlier spacecraft could not land on Earth. They had to crash into the ocean where ships picked them up from the water.

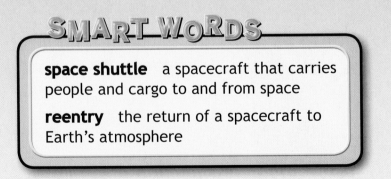

## SMART WORDS

**space shuttle**   a spacecraft that carries people and cargo to and from space

**reentry**   the return of a spacecraft to Earth's atmosphere

Imagine you are in the shuttle ready for take off. You hear the countdown. On "zero," the solid rocket boosters fire. Soon you are high above the ocean! The boosters drop off. The main engines fire. The external fuel tank drops off. You are in orbit!

Then you are ready to return to Earth. **Reentry** could be a problem. Most objects burn up when they pass through Earth's atmosphere. But special materials on the shuttle protect it from the heat. Now you are ready to glide in for a smooth landing!

External fuel tank

Solid rocket boosters

Shuttle

# To Go Where No Human Has Gone Before

People have traveled to the moon. They have lived in space for months. But, there are places we cannot go yet. Space is a big place. It is filled with danger. But that doesn't stop people from wanting to explore!

A **space probe** is an unmanned spacecraft sent into space to do research. Space probes carry cameras and special instruments. They collect data about planets, moons, and other objects. These tools have given us a close-up view of all the planets in our solar system. They have landed on asteroids! They have flown by comets!

The *Galileo* space probe was launched in 1989. It entered Jupiter's atmosphere in 1995. It observed Jupiter for almost eight years before crashing into the surface of the planet in 2003.

14

Some satellites are used for mapping Earth's surface. You can now view almost any location on Earth on your computer!

Space exploration began with artificial satellites. An **artificial satellite** is a man-made object that orbits Earth or other planets. The first one was launched in 1957 and was called *Sputnik I*. Thousands of satellites have been launched into orbit since then.

Satellites have many uses. Some study Earth or other planets. Others are used for cell phones and television broadcasts. Satellites are also used for navigation, weather, and military support.

## SMART WORDS

**space probe**   an unmanned spacecraft sent into space to do research

**artificial satellite**   a man-made object that orbits Earth or other planets to collect information

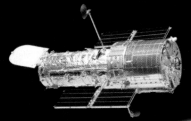

The Hubble Space Telescope has sent back amazing pictures from space.

## Hubble Space Telescope

Imagine having eyes in the sky! The **Hubble Space Telescope** is our eyes in space. It is one of the world's most powerful space telescopes and cameras. It sends pictures from space back to Earth. These pictures let us see the far reaches of space — things we never could have imagined.

The Hubble Space Telescope has taken pictures of stars forming in space. It has even taken pictures of the cores of distant galaxies. These pictures amaze everyone who sees them!

The Hubble Space Telescope is helping us explore the universe. The universe is everything throughout all of space. The universe is larger than we can even know. Scientists have proven that the universe is constantly growing! They can use information from the Hubble telescope to estimate the size of the universe. They can also tell how quickly the universe is expanding.

The Hubble Space Telescope often needs repairs. It also needs routine maintenance. Several space shuttle missions have been launched to work on the telescope.

The Hubble Space Telescope took this picture. It shows stars forming from gas and dust.

## SMART WORDS

**Hubble Space Telescope**   a space telescope that takes pictures of distant areas in space

**universe**   everything throughout space

# Mission to Mars

Mars is our next-door neighbor in space. People have always wondered about this planet. The first spacecraft to successfully reach Mars was sent in 1964. It took pictures of a red dusty landscape. In movies and stories, the word "Martian" has been used to mean imaginary space beings. But we know for sure that no real Martians ever existed on Mars.

Some scientists think they have found proof of life on Mars, though! Evidence of microscopic organisms has led some scientists to believe that there was once life on Mars.

Pictures from Mars show a dry, rocky surface. The surface is covered by a rusty dust. The dust gives the planet a reddish color.

The Mars Rover *Spirit* began its mission to Mars in 2003.

In recent years, **rovers** have been sent to explore Mars. Rovers are unmanned vehicles that drive across the surface of the planet. The rovers collect data about the soil and rocks. The data suggests that water once flowed on Mars.

Humans cannot yet travel to Mars. But they can control the rovers on the planet. Rovers work because of **teleoperation**. People control the rovers from Earth with remote controls. These are not toy cars! They cost millions of dollars.

## SMART WORDS

**rover**  an unmanned vehicle that drives across the surface of a planet

**teleoperation**  control of a machine by remote control from another place

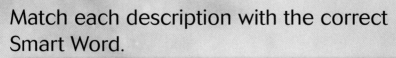
Match each description with the correct Smart Word.

| rover | teleoperation | artificial satellite |
| Hubble Space Telescope | reentry | |
| space probe | space shuttle | universe |

1. I am everything throughout all of space.

2. I am a space telescope that takes pictures of distant areas in space.

3. I am a man-made object that orbits Earth or other planets to collect information.

4. I am a spacecraft that carries people and cargo to and from space.

5. I am an unmanned spacecraft sent into space to do research.

6. I am a vehicle that has traveled on the surface of Mars.

7. I describe when a spacecraft returns to Earth's atmosphere.

8. I explain how machines are controlled with remote control.

Answers on page 32

# Talk Like a Scientist

Talk about the different ways we learn about what lies beyond Earth. Use Smart Words to tell your story.

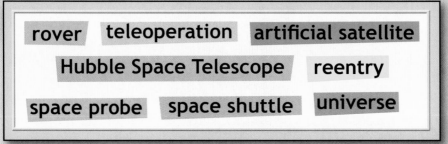

# SMART FACTS

## Did You Know?

Romans gave the planet the name Mars. Egyptians called the planet "Her Desher," which means "The Red One," since it reminded them of blood. It is really iron oxide, or rust.

## That's Amazing

Mars can have terrible dust storms. The winds can be about 120 miles (190 kilometers) per hour and last for weeks at a time.

NASA's *Phoenix Mars Lander* touched down on Mars in 2008. It studies the planet and sends information to scientists on Earth.

## Incredible Fact

Scientists have looked for water on Mars. But the atmosphere is too thin. Water cannot exist there as a liquid. It can only be found as water vapor or ice. However, gullies on the planet's surface suggest that water may have once flowed there.

# Chapter 3

# Living in Space!

Would you like to live in space?

Some scientists do just that! They work on the **International Space Station**. It is a huge research laboratory that orbits in space above Earth's surface. Scientists ride to work in a space shuttle instead of in a car or bus. When they arrive, the space shuttle hooks onto the space station. The scientists busily unload cargo and supplies. They must bring everything they need to live and work in space.

Scientists live and work on the space station. They may take a space walk to make repairs.

Scientists on the International Space Station
have to learn to sleep in space!

**Gravity** is the force of attraction between all
objects. It is what keeps our feet firmly planted
on Earth. The farther you get from Earth, the
weaker the force of gravity becomes. The
International Space Station orbits far above
Earth. It has very weak gravity.

Scientists on the space station have to adjust
to living with little gravity. They have to tie
themselves into bed! If they didn't, they would
float above it. As you can imagine, going to
the bathroom is a tricky business!

## SMART WORDS

**International Space Station**   a large research
laboratory that orbits Earth

**gravity**   the force of attraction between all objects

# Home, Home on the Moon!

Most astronauts stay at the International Space Station for about six months. Muscles get weak if people live in low gravity too long. However, some Russian astronauts have stayed in space for a year. Is it possible that someday people will live on the moon or some other planet for even longer? Maybe a lifetime?

Imagine going out at night and looking up at Earth! **Space colonization** is the idea of building human settlements outside of Earth. A space settlement would have to be airtight. It would have to hold air so humans could breathe.

This is a model of what a space colony might look like.

United States

Imagine living in a space colony. Your family lives in a home on the moon! You go to moon school. Your parents work mining the resources on the moon. The moon does not have oxygen, and water is very limited. So air and water have to be recycled.

Food is grown in large greenhouses. Conditions must be carefully controlled. Plants produce oxygen and use carbon dioxide. The greenhouses are an important part of controlling the atmosphere. Is this all just science fiction? It will probably really happen someday in the future!

## SMART WORD

**space colonization** the building of human settlements outside of Earth

# The Future of Space Science

Scientists also think about interplanetary travel. Interplanetary travel means travel between the planets. Space colonies could be launch sites for travel to other planets. They could also be used for space research.

The study of life in the universe is called astrobiology. Scientists are looking for planets that might support life. They are looking for planets with water and air. They are also looking for places with temperatures similar to Earth's. Maybe someday people like us will call these planets home!

## SMART WORDS

**interplanetary** between planets

**astrobiology** the study of life in the universe

**nuclear propulsion** a way to move a spacecraft forward quickly with a strong blast of fuel

Scientists also want to travel to places that are too far away to travel to today. **Nuclear propulsion** is a way to move a spacecraft forward very quickly. It uses a strong blast of fuel. This could allow a spacecraft to go places that are too far to reach with today's rockets. Where could we go if we could get there? How big is the universe, anyway? Scientists are excited to explore space and find the answers.

Kepler-11 is a star. It is similar to our star, the sun. Scientists have discovered six planets orbiting it.

# Use your SMART WORDS

Match each description with the correct Smart Word.

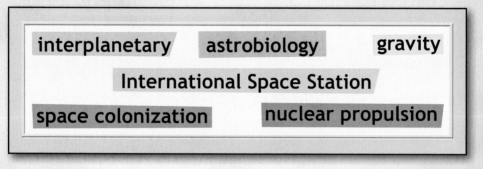

interplanetary     astrobiology          gravity

International Space Station

space colonization          nuclear propulsion

1. a way to move a spacecraft forward quickly with a strong blast of fuel

2. a large research laboratory that orbits Earth

3. between planets

4. the building of human settlements outside of Earth

5. the study of life in the universe

6. the force of attraction between all objects

Answers on page 32

## Talk Like a Scientist

Describe how you would build a space colony. Use your Smart Words to talk about how you would travel there, and how you would get everything needed to survive.

LAB

# SMART FACTS

## Did You Know?

The space station Mir was made of seven different modules. Over a ten-year period, different parts were brought to the space station and assembled.

## It's Amazing

After fifteen years in orbit, Mir was sent crashing to Earth. Most of it burned up as it passed through Earth's atmosphere, but chunks of debris fell into the Pacific Ocean.

## Incredible Fact

To get sleep, the crew on Mir had to cover the windows to create darkness. Orbiting above Earth, there were sixteen sunsets and sunrises a day!

# Glossary

**artificial satellite**  a man-made object that orbits Earth or other planets to collect information

**astrobiology**  the study of life in the universe

**astronaut**  a person who is trained to travel in space

**astronomy**  the study of space and objects in space

**force**  a push or pull that acts on an object

**gravity**  the force of attraction between all objects

**Hubble Space Telescope**  a space telescope that takes pictures of distant areas in space

**International Space Station**  a large research laboratory that orbits Earth

**interplanetary**  between planets

**nuclear propulsion**  a way to move a spacecraft forward quickly with a strong blast of fuel

**reentry**  the return of a spacecraft to Earth's atmosphere

**robot**   a machine that can do tasks for people

**rocket**   a type of engine that burns fuel and pushes hot gases out one end to move

**rover**   an unmanned vehicle that drives across the surface of a planet

**space colonization**   the building of human settlements outside of Earth

**space probe**   an unmanned spacecraft sent into space to do research

**space shuttle**   a spacecraft that carries people and cargo to and from space

**teleoperation**   control of a machine by remote control from another place

**telescope**   a tool that makes faraway objects appear closer

**universe**   everything throughout space

# Index

## SMART WORDS Answer Key

**Page 10**
1. rocket,  2. astronomy,  3. force,  4. astronaut,  5. telescope,
6. robot

**Page 20**
1. universe,  2. Hubble Space Telescope,  3. artificial satellite,
4. space shuttle,  5. space probe,  6. rover,  7. reentry,
8. teleoperation

**Page 28**
1. nuclear propulsion,  2. International Space Station,
3. interplanetary,  4. space colonization,  5. astrobiology,
6. gravity